Duck
NO PARKING

13

I EXPECT TO PASS THROUGH
THIS WORLD BUT ONCE;
ANY GOOD THING THEREFORE
THAT I CAN DO, OR ANY
KINDNESS THAT I CAN SHOW
TO ANY FELLOW-CREATURE,
LET ME DO IT NOW; LET ME
NOT DEFER OR NEGLECT IT,
FOR I SHALL NOT PASS THIS
WAY AGAIN.

22

Check out my other books avaiable.

CREATIVE CAKES

BEAUTIFUL CAKES

MISC RAMBLING

FLOWER PICTURES

BEAUTIFUL FLOWERS

MISC RAMBLING

RICHMOND VA

CITY OF RICHMOND

MISC RAMBLING

NASHVILLE TN

ARCHITECTURE DOWNTOWN

MISC RAMBLING

CHARLESTON

CHARLESTON SC

MISC RAMBLING

THE BATTERY

CHARLESTON STATUE

MISC RAMBLING

NEW BERN NC

TRYON PALACE
NORTH CAROLINA HISTORY
CENTER & MORE!

MISC RAMBLING

The end.